T0400647

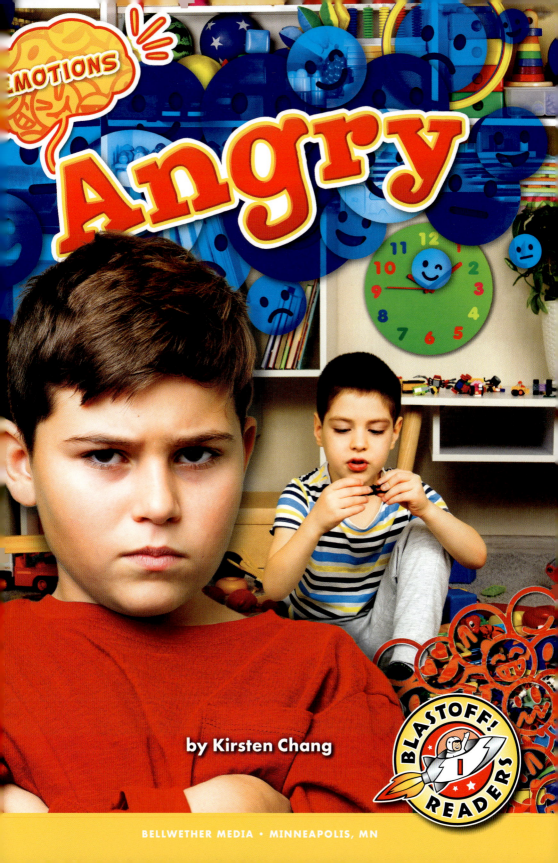

EMOTIONS

Angry

by Kirsten Chang

BLASTOFF! READERS

BELLWETHER MEDIA • MINNEAPOLIS, MN

Blastoff! Readers are carefully developed by literacy experts to build reading stamina and move students toward fluency by combining standards-based content with developmentally appropriate text.

Level 1 provides the most support through repetition of high-frequency words, light text, predictable sentence patterns, and strong visual support.

Level 2 offers early readers a bit more challenge through varied sentences, increased text load, and text-supportive special features.

Level 3 advances early-fluent readers toward fluency through increased text load, less reliance on photos, advancing concepts, longer sentences, and more complex special features.

★ **Blastoff! Universe**

Reading Level

Grade
K

Grades
1–3

Grade
4

This edition first published in 2025 by Bellwether Media, Inc.

No part of this publication may be reproduced in whole or in part without written permission of the publisher. For information regarding permission, write to Bellwether Media, Inc., Attention: Permissions Department, 6012 Blue Circle Drive, Minnetonka, MN 55343.

Library of Congress Cataloging-in-Publication Data

LC record for Angry available at: https://lccn.loc.gov/2024014729

Editor: Rebecca Sabelko   Designer: Andrea Schneider

Printed in the United States of America, North Mankato, MN.

Table of Contents

Some kids are
playing a game.
They will not
let Ava play.
Ava feels angry.

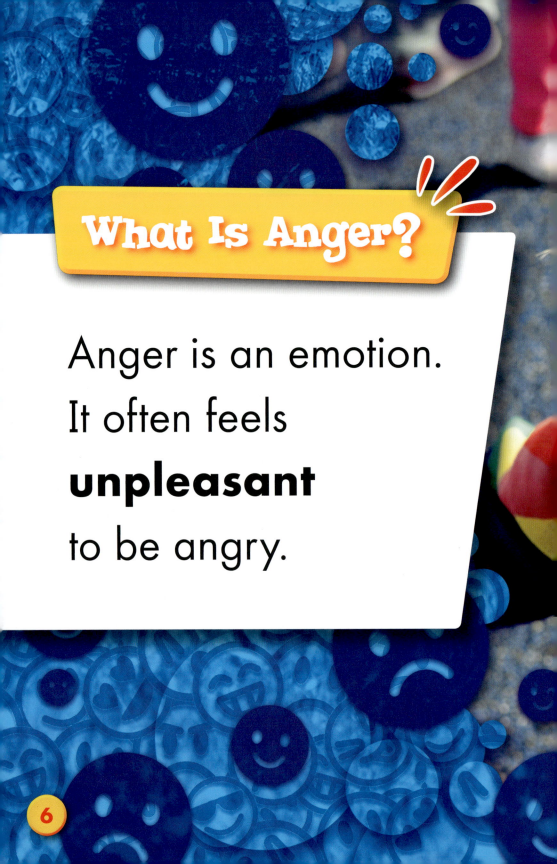

What Is Anger?

Anger is an emotion.
It often feels
unpleasant
to be angry.

Mad and upset
are other words
for angry.
Frustrated also
means angry.

Sometimes things seem unfair.
Olivia wants candy.
Her mom said no.
Olivia gets angry.

Why Are You Angry?

getting left out

being told no

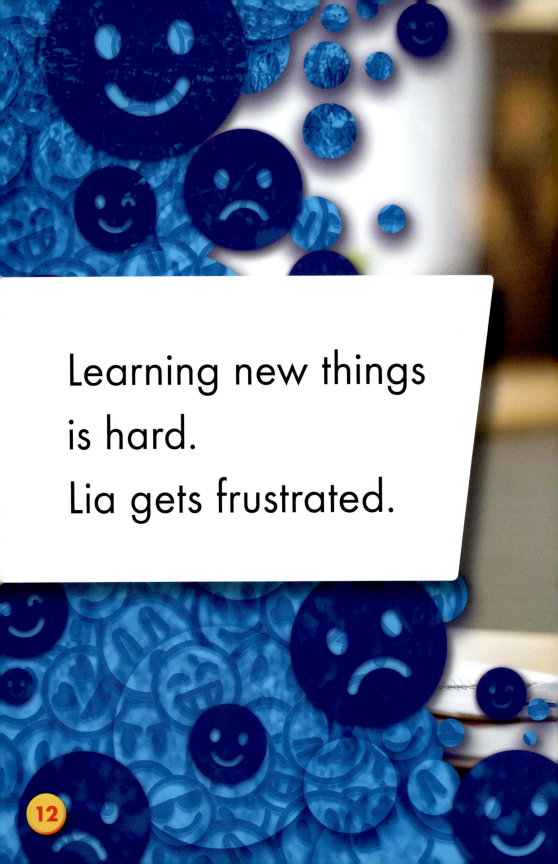

Learning new things
is hard.
Lia gets frustrated.

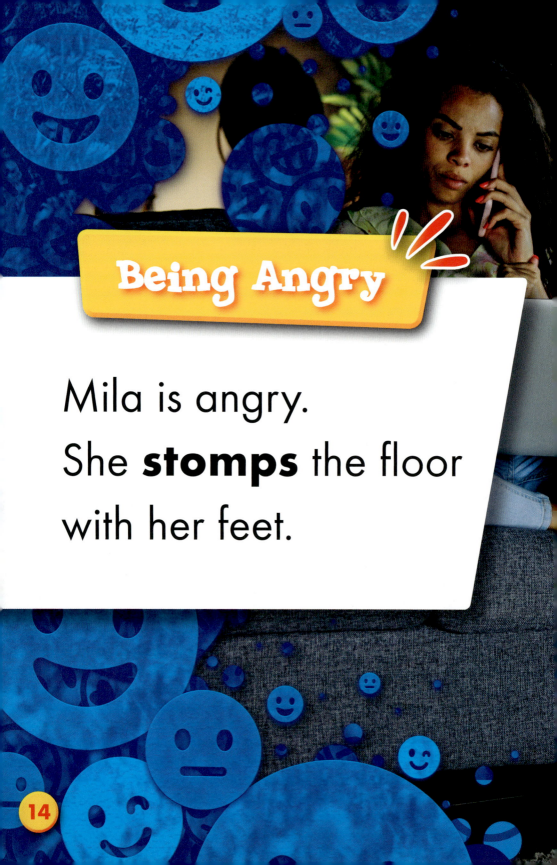

Being Angry

Mila is angry.
She **stomps** the floor
with her feet.

stomping
foot

15

Ella is upset.
She starts to cry.

16

17

RJ feels hot
when he is mad.
His face turns red.
He gets **sweaty**.

sweat →

Identify Anger

stomping

crying

sweating

19

Take a break
when you feel angry.
Breathe deeply.
You will soon feel calm.

What makes you feel angry?

21

Glossary

frustrated

feeling unhappy when things do not go the way you want

sweaty

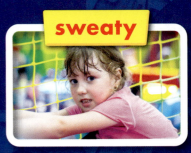

having a wet feeling on the skin caused by sweat

stomps

hits the ground hard with feet

unpleasant

not nice

To Learn More

AT THE LIBRARY

Atwood, Megan. *Mason the Moose Feels Mad*. Minneapolis, Minn.: Jump!, 2024.

Chang, Kirsten. *Understanding Emotions*. Minneapolis, Minn.: Bellwether Media, 2022.

Culliford, Amy. *Angry*. New York, N.Y.: Crabtree Publishing, 2021.

ON THE WEB

FACTSURFER

Factsurfer.com gives you a safe, fun way to find more information.

1. Go to www.factsurfer.com.

2. Enter "angry" into the search box and click Q.

3. Select your book cover to see a list of related content.

Index